ALLY GALAXY
everyone is different

ALLY GALAXY
everyone is different

This is a work of fiction. Names, characters, places, and incidents either are the products of author imagination or are used fictitiously, and any resemblance to actual persons, living or dead, business establishments, events, or locales is entirely coincidental.

Copyright ©2018 Michael Szczurko
www.allygalaxy.com

Illustrated by,
Cathy Bolio

All rights reserved. This book is licensed to the original purchaser only. Duplication or distribution via any means is illegal and a violation of international copyright law, subject to criminal prosecution and upon conviction, fines, and/or imprisonment. Any eBook format cannot be legally loaned or given to others. No part of this book may be reproduced or transmitted in any form or by any means, electronic, or mechanical, including photocopying, recording, or by any information storage and retrieval system, without the written permission of the Publisher, except where permitted by law. To request permission and all other inquiries, contact Michael Szczurko, allygalaxybook@gmail.com, or http://www.allygalaxy.com/.

Library of Congress Control Number: 2018906892

ISBN 978-1-7324372-0-3

ALLY GALAXY
everyone is different

by,
michael szczurko & johnna bond

for lincoln, our little happy boy

MY NAME IS ALLY GALAXY
MY LIFE IS ABOUT TO CHANGE
I AM MOVING TO ANOTHER PLANET
I KNOW IT SOUNDS STRANGE

GOODBYE TO MY FRIENDS
GOODBYE TO MY TOWN
GOODBYE TO MR. LANCY
AND HIS OVERSIZED FROWN

I'VE SEEN ONES WITH HORNS
AND ONES WITH SPOTS
I'VE EVEN SEEN ONE
ALL TIED UP IN KNOTS

I SAW ONE FAST AS LIGHTNING
ANOTHER SLOW AS A SNAIL
WITH AN ANVIL ON IT'S BACK
AND A PAINFUL HANGNAIL

HORNS THAT ARE TWISTY
AND TAILS THAT ARE STRAIGHT

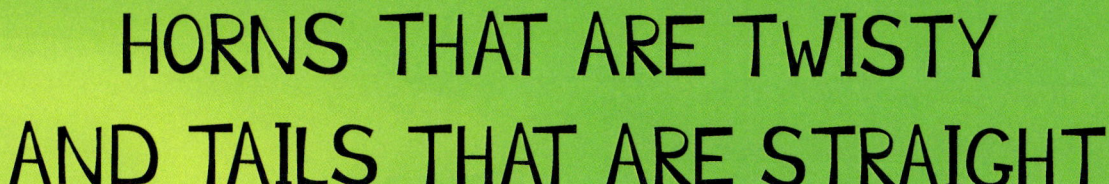

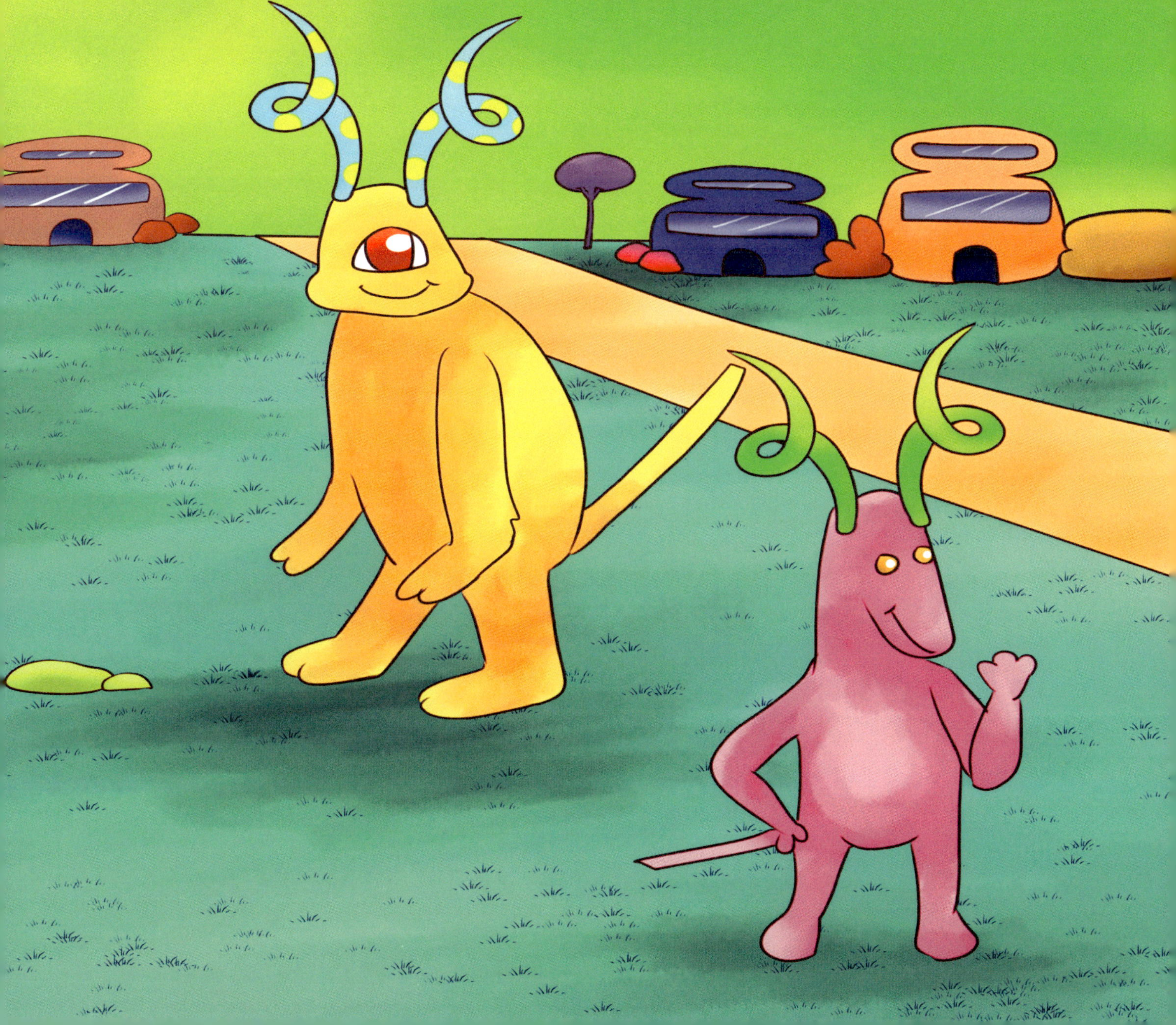

I THOUGHT WE WERE DIFFERENT

SO I EXCLAIM...